S.T.R.I.V.E

STRIVE TO REACH IMPOSSIBLE VISIONS EVERYDAY

for

GREATNESS

MOTIVATION IN YOUR OWN IMAGE

SWALLOW PUBLISHING

PRAISE FOR DR. NIGEL L. WALKER

As a public speaker and a performer, there are three words that describe Nigel Walker. Innovative. Informative. Inspiring. From giving motivational speeches, to performing original compositions of rap and spoken word, Nigel elevates the minds and souls of all who are blessed to hear his voice.

– Dr. J. Lamar Hardwick
Pastor and Author

I have observed Nigel's instruction and performances on multiple occasions over the last three years. Many committed academics are not that entertaining while many energetic entertainers lack academic expertise. Nigel is both an extraordinary entertainer and an asset to public education in multiple curriculum areas. His performers can stir positive emotions among a crowd of 800 while his teaching can be student-centered to reach all learners. I am honored to work with him and proud to call him a friend.

– Dr. Clay Hildebrand
Educator

Nigel Walker is an amazing speaker. He engages his audience and speaks to them on a level to which they can relate. He is both inspiring and honest in his delivery sharing personal experiences and allowing insight into who is while delivering his message.

– Sheree Thomas
Owner at Stage Presents

Nigel is one of the most passionate, professional, and poised speakers I've seen. He is relevant with his message, no matter your age.

– Bobbie Harrington

Nigel spoke at two amazing events that I facilitated as Lyceum chair as a member of SGA at Georgia Perimeter College. The first event was "Summer Solstice", and due to a number of student requests, we invited him back to speak at "Winter Solstice" He is an amazing, insightful and engaging speaker.

– Martha C. Wallace

Your performances are epic! They're emotionally driven and they incorporate facts with real world knowledge. Students in all socioeconomic brackets can learn from and relate to your take on life and the perpetuation of generations keeping themselves from prospering. Poetry at its best, but it is much more than that. It's a plea for kids to understand that they have power over their own education and their own circumstances.

– L. M. Jones
Former Educator

Dr. Nigel Walker's is a participant at Long Cane Middle School's Black History Program. For the past three years he has prepared and delivered an original poetic piece with vigor and much enthusiasm to a crowd of 11–14 year-olds that respond with excitement and a new perspective on modern issues. There isn't another one like Mr. Walker.

– Sonya Brown
Educator

This book is dedicated to my mother, Jacqueline Walker.

I dedicate everything to her because she is the source of my life and success. All of my determination and drive originates in her words and actions, which were ingrained in me. I only hope that one day, something that I have dedicated to her is fruitful in its value to reflect the value I place in her being my mother.

TABLE OF CONTENTS

FOREWORD

In this foreword, I will be telling you about some of the chapters that I absolutely loved, but before I do, I just want to say that I am honored and it gave me great pleasure for my role model for a long time now, Dr. Nigel Walker, to allow me to write the foreword for this work. It gave me so much insight on how to "Seek To Reach Impossible Visions Every day for Greatness." You don't see adolescents doing these kinds of things, so I am humbled, grateful, and blessed to be doing this.

The first chapter I loved was the "Great Minds" chapter. This chapter connected to me because if the chaos in 2020 has afforded us anything, it's revolutionary thinking. During this pandemic of COVID-19 and the pandemic of civil unrest, I have learned that it is our time to start challenging models across every production. The real lesson that I got from this chapter was that we must use this moment to take a seat at the table, and if the table isn't making life better for your generation, shake it — or better yet, break it down and build a new one. Fortunately, my generation is doing that right now because we are tired of being on the menu and not being able to sit at the table.

When I read the chapters "Great Power" and "Great Responsibility," I put those two chapters because I immediately thought of the quote by Spider-Man that says, "With great power lies great responsibility." That quote is basically saying, "If you have the ability to do something, make sure that you do it for the good of others." When I think of the quote and the meaning, I think of Luke 12:48, which says, "From everyone who has been given much, much will be demanded; and from the one who has been entrusted with much, much more will be asked." If you have heard that line of wisdom, you know it means we are held responsible for what we have. If we have been blessed with talents, wealth, knowledge, time, and the like, it is expected that we benefit others. So while we're in these two pandemics, we must find out how we can benefit others to make the world a better place.

The chapter "Great Expectations" really stuck out to me because there are 5 principles that Dr. Walker wrote and one of them is that "I must show empathy/compassion." What I learned from that is that as creative people, our job is to document the world through empathetic and compassionate eyes. We're given a unique lens to capture pain, vitality, and everything in between, with fine distinction. Yes, the world appears to be in a state of darkness, but there is hope, and it lies in those who have the ability to manifest dreams.

Everyone has their own set goal that they strive to reach in their lifetime; it's what makes life have purpose. Every day we work to do something with our lives, to be successful. Reaching these goals and being successful in life does not come easy. Nothing you want comes overnight; it is retained with a set mind on that goal and the desire to work to reach that goal. I believe that success comes from hard work and determination. My mom is my role model of what I believe; she is the very definition of a determined, hardworking adult. She does not believe in giving up, she works hard to give her family a better life. To give me and my sister a stable home, to give us the chance to reach out for our own success is not an easy job, but I believe she has already accomplished this. I have a great life and I am doing things like this because of her, because of what she has already provided for me. She reaches for success and also motivates my sister and I to reach for our own goals, to strive to be great. She is what drives me to want to be successful and to be someone who can contribute to society and to make my family proud. Dr. Martin Luther King, Jr. is also my role model. Even though he's not here anymore, his legacy lives on and I look up to him. Not because of how famous and successful he was, but because of how determined he was to help Black people be treated equally and how hard he worked to do it. He went from skipping ninth grade and not graduating to be a Baptist minister and social activist. He displayed the power of hard work and determination through his work. The secret to greatness lies in the small actions we each take every day. Although we won't all be recognized by history, each of us is capable of achieving greatness through our everyday actions. Most of the good in the world is built on the accumulated efforts of ordinary people doing small things in a great way.

This book left me amazed and speechless. It really showed me how important it is to strive for greatness. This book will forever be in my personal tool kit of life and I hope it will be in yours also. With that being said, I believe God has a purpose for everyone in this world. Whatever your purpose is, it does not come easy. To be successful, to fulfill your purpose, you must be willing to work hard and to stay determined, to **S.T.R.I.V.E. for Greatness.** This book shows you how to do just that.

Khamani Philpotts
High School Class of 2022
National Society of High School Scholars

INTRODUCTION

You define who you are by learning and knowing what you want to do and be. The pursuit of that knowledge creates the image that others see. Though your path should not give in to the influence of others, it is notable to realize that it is the others who will build your monument. So when you decide what path you take, decide the one from which history is written. Strive for greatness. Seek to reach impossible visions every day. Be the example of what others desire to be. Be the master of your success and the model for others. Take any and all opportunities to step one foot ahead of the trend and set a new trend. Be a trendsetter.

The purpose of this book is to break down the specifics of how to arrive at the peak of your greatness. The first step was picking up this work. Your first vision involves your desire to be great, as evidenced in the reading of this title and following through with its purchase. This purchase was important. This purchase was significant. Congratulations on your first feeling of striving for greatness. This purchase shows that your mindset is already in a place that brings fear and anxiety to many, and maybe it's even a little scary to you, but proceeding despite the fear will prove valuable in the end.

Let the year 2020 tell it: life has presented a perfect stage for finding one's path of greatness through fear and uncertainty. With events that have taken place—as people all have described as unprecedented, difficult, and even the end times—we all found ourselves in a state of confusion and discomfort. One could describe it in cinematic terms. The spread of a virus in a novel pandemic, historic demonstrations due to elevated racial tensions, and monumental economic uncertainty and despair— not to mention shortages of food and supplies of epic proportions at times. But as many leaders charged, it was times like those where an equal level of unprecedented strength and resolve could also be found.

It was in those times where the most unlikely heroes and saviors revealed their qualities. It was in those times where the pages of history were stroked with freshly inked lines of iconic deeds. It was where greatness waited to be discovered.

Greatness is as rare, yet abundant as the precious elements that lie beneath the layers of the earth, only to be discovered by those who dare to excavate them. And when you look at it, every person privileged to walk the earth has an equal opportunity to decide if he or she wants to be a prospector of greatness. The conscious choice to begin the journey, get down and dirty, and take on the painstaking labor to reach the treasures that lie beneath is what separated those who discovered from those who yielded to the challenge.

Like the prospectors, now is the perfect time for us to dig deep and discover our internal desires and drive to walk into unprecedented times with boldness, to walk into the uncharted territory with confidence. Olympic champion Wilma Rudolph once said, "Never underestimate the power of dreams and the influence of the human spirit. We are all the same in this notion:

The potential for greatness lives within each of us." Now is the perfect time to reach impossible visions and strive for greatness.

It has always been said that if your dreams or goals do not scare you, they are not big enough. Impossible visions are those big dreams we all formulate in moments of heightened motivation, but sometimes lose in the struggles of everyday life. Seeking those impossible visions every day gives us a renewed passion to work hard every day, chipping away at the terrain until we reach that treasure of greatness.

The drive to reach impossible visions has to come from within us. We must be motivated in our own image. The term "motivation in your own image" refers to seeking the model of those who you label as "great," but modifying those qualities to make them personal to you. Carve your own path in greatness. Be motivated to create your unique image of greatness. We hear multiple messages all the time that are aimed to inspire us and light the fire, but the fire cannot be lit by others. We must find within ourselves the match to spark the desire to take the journey. That match has to be our thinking.

In an intro to an album by hip hop group Dead Prez, the narrator says, "My mind is where I make my plan, the world is where I take my stand." This quote has always stayed with me as a reminder of the order of business involved in striving for greatness. The mind is the blueprint, where the access to knowledge of strengths, beliefs, and values all reside as the ingredients to the plan. To strike the match, we must establish the mindset for greatness.

S.T.R.I.V.E FOR GREATNESS

If you break down the word "mindset," it can be seen as the literal interpretation that the mind is set. I define mindset as the decision of what strengths, beliefs, and values one is about set into action. It is the choice of what one values and believes in, and what knowledge one has that will inform the decision to seek impossible visions every day—to strive for greatness. Our mindset also gauges the motivation we have, which can be highly influenced by our self-image.

In this book, we will explore how to access the knowledge of strengths, beliefs, and values it takes to strive for greatness. We will begin with the mindset, discovering my "why" through great minds of history as sources of establishing a mindset of greatness. Subsequently, we will explore the great power, great responsibility, and great expectations associated with seeking to reach impossible visions every day. We will discuss the actions necessary to strive for greatness. Finally, we will discover how the content shared throughout this book was put into the context of my personal biography, giving clinical evidence to my claims. The framework of the book is designed to develop a personal identification that allows the reader establish a self-image of greatness needed to initiate the journey to reach impossible visions. The decision to step out on such faith takes mountains of courage and can be easily deterred by the vision of others. So the structure of this book is to help overcome the apprehensions that can hinder one from seeking the impossible visions. However, I am going to interject a brief explanation for the Strive Chain before we get into the main content.

THE STRIVE CHAIN

Before we go into serious discussion, let me address one little element of my platform: The Strive Chain. The look of the Strive Chain may be all too familiar to you, resembling the popular sports relic, the Turnover Chain.

Popularized by the University of Miami, the Turnover Chain was intended as an incentive to motivate football players on the team to achieve great feats of skill. Whenever they caused a takeaway, they were awarded the coveted Turnover Chain. Its popularity exploded exponentially and took many forms, such as wrestling championship belts and thrones, among other representations.

In a report by Mark Richt, Miami's head coach at the time, he stated that there was more to it than celebrating the turnover itself. They were also celebrating a movement. Although I throw in the disclaimer that I'm not a diehard fan of the U, the significance of the Turnover Chain has always stuck with me and ultimately led me to use a version of a chain as part of my platform. My thinking took me into areas of celebrations, processes, movements, and even the realm of cultural relevance.

It is commonly seen that the wearing of a large gold chain is most closely connected to hip hop/rap culture to signify wealth. In hip hop culture, the ceremony of awarding an artist a gold chain with the record label logo on it was a rite of passage in the music industry. Even dating back to ancient times, the reception of riches was symbolic of an achieved status. Though the whole ritual has in a sense been trivialized or even stereotyped in today's society, I could not help but latch on to one component — the rite of passage.

I believe that the message is two-fold. The first message is celebrate the wins whether they are big or small. The small wins can be a game changer. The big wins can manifest as a rite of passage; a point I believe Coach Richt aimed for as well, because it elevates the action beyond a materialistic acquisition or a point of status to the commencement of greatness. It does not merely include the riches; it also includes the intrinsically rewarded feelings of self-actualization, of self-esteem, and of self-worth.

As I thought about those qualities of motivation, I asked myself why such an effective approach should be limited to such mainstream institutions as popular sports and music. Should we not want individuals to experience those same feelings upon achieving personal, professional, or even academic goals? So, as part of my platform—as I spoke to students, young adults, and any individual about seeking to reach impossible visions every day in order to strive for greatness—I decided to adopt the Strive Chain.

As the Turnover Chain was looked upon as an ultimate motivator to athletes and musicians, the Strive Chain can be viewed as an ultimate motivator in the area of academic achievement, as well as personal and professional goal setting. It is also a very relatable symbol from a culturally relevant standpoint. The simple message is this: Celebrate the wins! They can be a small win all the way up to the celebration of a rite of passage into greatness. From the culmination of the previously stated ideas, the Strive Chain was born!

GREAT MINDS

The old saying is that great minds think alike. So in order to achieve greatness, one must think like the greats. Many great minds have come and gone in the world, so it is important to narrow the focus to those who match the image of greatness we wish to mimic. We are always told that we can be anything we want to be in life, and the greats show us that there are those who match up with our mindset and even our beliefs and background. We must seek to find the model that allows us to turn their values into our principles, their words into our mantra, and their actions into our lifestyle. There is one caveat that I will add to "Great Minds." They have uniquely earned their title by standing out as the example of what it looks like to be great. They sought the impossible visions and achieved incomparable outcomes. So it is important to note that though we want to study their greatness and develop the qualities that made them great, we also have to remember that we have our own unique existence and experiences. We must take the clay that is the qualities of greatness and mold them into our personal representation. The journey to greatness is not only about taking lessons from those who came before us, it is also about internalizing the beliefs and values to cultivate a mindset to seek the impossible visions[1]. We must create our own unique image and become motivated in constructing own unique story of greatness.

S.T.R.I.V.E FOR GREATNESS

I have striven to follow the greats and hope to pay it forward in the future. In doing so, I have contemplated about why it is important for me to be a role model for success and achievement; and even more, I also think about why anyone else should care. Looking at and trying to understand the contributions of the great minds of my personal inspiration, I have concluded that in some form or fashion, they worked toward the greater good of society and it is my duty as a contributing member of society to do the same. One might question how much of an influence and individual can have on the greater good of society, but in my experience, I have seen my own personal story and motivation have somewhat a domino effect on others to seek impossible visions. My efforts did not come through the gift of any specific privilege, it came through my decision to seek the opportunities that others had and capitalize when others did not. I fought for equal opportunities and access for myself and sharing my stories gave others ideas about how to do the same. After defining my purpose, I began to look for "Great Minds" that shared similar stories of which I could model. It was no surprise that the Great Minds of whom inspired me the most were those involved in seeking what seems to be an impossible vision in our society today, and that is social justice.

Social justice is defined as justice in terms of the equal distribution of wealth, opportunities, and privileges within a society. From a personal standpoint, I reflect upon a background of poverty, public housing, and being raised in a single-parent family with seven other siblings. I reflect upon the generations of my family members living in the same public housing, the generational poverty, and dream of having the wealth, opportunities, and privileges that could change my situation. I look to history and how opportunities and barriers for success today still exist in similar patterns for entire races of people. I particularly look to the history of African Americans as it is filled experiences of individuals and groups as a whole striving to obtain opportunities and access to basic freedoms and liberties equal to other individuals and groups around them. What have I learned has become part of the foundation of my motivation to seek to reach impossible visions every day, and to strive for greatness.

I've learned that, if I want to be great and if I want to be successful, I must have a mindset of overcoming, as did those who shared my ancestry in the past. This is why history is part of my platform. My intent is not to present a history lesson—even though I do hold a doctorate in education and stay ready to teach—the point of this chapter is to paint a picture of motivation behind my vision to strive for greatness, giving others a vision map to follow grounded in a socio-historical context.

It is important to know the names, faces, and details of those we emulate. We can all agree that we owe much to figures such as Dr. Martin Luther King, Jr., Rosa Parks, George Washington Carver, W.E.B. Dubois, and countless others. We often pay them homage for their significant work. It is equally important to take the significance of their work and internalize it to establish our own personal mindset for success, which in turn creates the notion to "think alike." In the interest of simplicity, I will focus on the significance of the work that was done during pivotal historical time periods that helped construct my personal vision map to greatness.

First, however, I ask again why anyone else should care, especially if they do not share my ethnic background. One might see this portion of the book as limiting, but allow me to elaborate on the purpose of the chapter. After all, the point of the book is to provide moments of motivation. The answer is simple—there is always a majority and a minority dynamic despite race, gender, economic status, or other subgroups. Many experiences could potentially leave any of us with a feeling of inferiority, where we have to fight and persevere to reach impossible visions and to be great at overcoming the situation. African American history teems with examples of values that that can become principles, words that can become mantras, and actions that can become lifestyles. African American history also is one of the most powerful resources to explore the issues dealing with views of humanity, the center point for becoming and being remembered as "great."

Equally important for those who are not of the same ethnicity is the significance of learning the stories of others. Greatness requires us to see through multiple lenses, so if the experience cannot be lived, the ability to relate can be learned. Those who don't have the experience can get a more accurate understanding of the history and systems of oppression, privilege, and inequality[2]. It helps those to navigate through a world of diversity in a positive manner and empower them to help society move towards a more shared vision of cultural values. Learning to relate builds empathy, which is a significant concept in striving for greatness, as I will discuss later.

To break down the "why" of my motivation, I started with historical perspectives, as I understood what impossible visions looked like through the lens of being an African American. I began to break down the underlying messages communicated in events and why it was important for historical figures to strive to achieve their historical accomplishments. Again, I share my rationale not as a history expert, but as my personal interpretation and internalization of history, pulling my "why" out of the historical context in my effort to think like the great minds before me. My conclusions were drawn from academic experiences and expertise, so the reader can be assured that my views have support and academic review.

To organize my train of thought, I reflected on three distinct time periods: the Antebellum Era and Slavery, the Civil Rights Era, and the 21st Century. They are painfully obvious and maybe a bit cliché, but that's the point. I want the motivation for others to be as simple and memorable, but as impactful as possible.

Within the three time periods, the patterns I found fell along the sub-contexts of general humanity and education.

Antebellum Era and Slavery

I will begin with slavery and explain why it is part of my "why" to strive for greatness. In all of the historical facts, figures, and information that I have read and heard over the years, two big ideas stick out to me—inequalities in education and humanity.

I have concluded that in general, there presided an unequal view of education and humanity between the enslaved and their masters. Even in literal terms, as outlined by the Three-Fifths Compromise of the Constitution, slaves were written in as three-fifths of a human and as property belonging to their owners. There is no greater direct example in the unequal view of humanity.

In my personal view, the motivation this era provides is to always strive to be more than what someone expects or assumes. In today's times, what someone expects or assumes is so frequently based on a person's actions that it is vital to start each day with a S.T.RI.V.E. mantra. It only takes one bad moment to wipe out a lifetime of good moments. Such can be seen with the recurrences of racism, which oftentimes aren't based on present actions, but past actions. Furthermore, it stems from the actions of others instead of the person to whom the racism is directed. The beauty of striving for greatness is that it can act like a water repellent and lessen the effects of racism when your positive actions are strong.

Holding multiple degrees in education, I have read into the second component of slavery far too many times. The unequal view of education has been documented since slaves were brought over to America. We all have read of the history of how slaves were denied the privilege of learning to read and write. Basically, slaves were denied education. Those who secretly planned and attempted to acquire education often were physically or mentally abused in an effort to thwart their goal.

Certain texts of that time period went as far as sharing the apparent sentiment among slave owners that "an educated negro was a dangerous negro." The motivation I received from this notion came from the obvious question: Why was there such a great effort to deny education to a group of people who were in the same lens viewed as less than fully human beings?

As I contemplated that question, I came up with my personal conclusion that there was (and still remains) a genuine fear of educated African Americans. The danger, in my humble opinion, is that education is a great equalizer, which inherently lessens the superiority of those who possess such a mindset. As I read into and studied the history of slavery and actions endured in such times, I believed that slave owners and the general dominant race in fact respected the threat of equal humanity enough to go to great lengths to keep the slaves uneducated, contained, and confined.

I am encouraged that when one seeks to reach impossible visions, he or she is relinquished from confinement and has the potential that is feared by many. Such a powerful vision!

Civil Rights Era

The struggles that resulted from the unequal views during slavery were perpetuated through subsequent decades. My personal conclusion is that we experienced many "second verse, same as the first" occasions.

During the Civil Rights Era, the same unequal views of humanity and education could be seen through the lens of the "Separate, But Equal" notion. The documentation of the times shows us a separation between white establishments and colored establishments, but equality between the two clearly was lacking. Placement of access and resources was definitely on opposite spectrums to the extreme, exposing a clear superiority and inferiority.

Disparities also became a huge issue within the education system, to the point that, much like during the time of slavery, African Americans faced physical and mental threats and abuse in their efforts to achieve equal access. The "Separate, But Equal" idea embodied the entire conflict rooted in the unequal views of humanity and education.

After drawing the conclusion that we are basically caught in a cultural cycle, I was motivated to be at least one agent of change to stop the cycle and create a new pattern. The pattern started with my waking up each day and carrying out at least one activity that put me in the equal view of others or at least put me a step closer to a grand vision that was equal or unmatched in superiority of the others. Not in the sense of a reversed role, but more in the sense of creating my own unique lane that is singularly attributed to my relentless efforts. To me, that defines greatness. It does not have to show superiority—instead, it shows unique efforts of achievement. Those efforts go beyond the typical or even the imaginable, forcing one to seek to reach impossible visions.

21st Century

The term "21st Century" is not only the literal delineation of where we sit in the markings of time, but it has also been associated as a term of advanced innovation in multiple realms of society. It alludes to advancements in technology as well as in education. It reflects an idea of progression and evolution into the future—on the surface.

As my personal and professional experience will reveal, however, we are still playing that same record from decades and centuries ago because the vision has not changed. The unequal views of humanity and education have also evolved and have been grounded within the boundaries of politics and community, which condones their existence.

An unequal view of humanity in recent times has brought about movements such as Black Lives Matter. Even mentioning the name can spark radically opposing views in a political and racial divide that creates as many problems as solutions. To avoid the point being missed, I want to focus on the visions.

The BLM movement was created from a concern that society holds an unequal view of humanity, creating a lack of sympathy and empathy for tragic events. The seriousness of the view should not be trivialized to a blame game, but more focused on clearing up the vision. The impossible vision in this situation is getting society as a whole to have a unified vision of humanity.

Before we dissect the first point, it is important to share the second aspect: an unequal view of education. My professional experience as an educator and in-depth research during my post-secondary education have led me to a common theme that is found in education—the achievement gap and the discipline gap.

The achievement gap is described as a result of decades of assessment outcomes where students of African American ethnicity excel at significantly lower rates than their classmates. Studies also have shown that African American students are disciplined and receive suspensions and expulsions at a rate that is nearly triple the rate of classmates. The existence of such a trend has led advocates to define the education system as a "school-to-prison pipeline." These alarming disparities also result in unequal access to education, because suspensions and expulsions remove students from the learning environment.

What are the impossible visions for the 21st Century? To remove all political ideology out of the equation, one must look at a vision for the future of humanity and education. I recall a local leader that headed the initiative on race reconciliation describing how racism and bigotry were perpetuated throughout time and history. He explained how stories are passed along and how these stories establish attitudes, and attitudes become culture. My interpretation is that the stories are the history and the passing is through education. History creates attitudes and culture, and history has shown an unequal view of humanity and education.

We must ask: With what types of history are we educating our students? This is why education should matter to African Americans. We should want our history to create positive attitudes and celebrate our culture. The purpose of public education is to create critical-thinking, problem-solving contributors to society who are skilled in knowledge acquisition, synthesis, and creation of solutions to unpredictable situations. Sift through all of the scholarly vocabulary and you get all the ingredients to bring about the equality and reconciliation we hope for. The stories are already there. What follows is what we choose to pass along—what attitudes we form from them, and what culture we establish. In short, the present state of a matter has been chosen.

Those who don't share stories of equality, unity, and reconciliation are choosing not to. This is what makes education important to everyone, regardless of race or ethnicity. When a story is passed to you and that story is not of equality, unity, and reconciliation, you have the power to change it or accept it. You have the power to be the voice of change or be part of the problem.

The vision for humanity, as previously stated, is a unified vision of equal humanity. We must look to the left and to right and see the person on each side of us as equal in our eyes. The vision for education is that education is a necessary tool to have choice, to overcome obstacles, and to reach goals.

When we buy an item that requires assembly, it comes with instructions. It is nearly impossible to wholly assemble most objects without instructions. Education instructs us in life. We learn the background through history, acquiring the tools to assemble a future through language, scientific method, and math computation. We advance our skills through electives and technology. Education gives us the instructions necessary to assemble a future.

The impossible vision is the universal respect for education that drives the passion to seek it. How does one achieve that drive? A drive to do something is like a force or a power, the scientific definitions of which are derived from a sense of movement and mechanics—of action. If we seek to reach impossible visions every day, we must take action. Striving for greatness takes deliberate work that starts with self. The power comes from within.

Achieving the impossible vision of equality of humanity and education must start with our own vision that we are equal. We must then take action to show that vision to others. If we begin with self and develop a positive vision of self-concept, self-determination, and self-discipline, we will begin to generate the power to be great.

After reading this chapter, I will seek to...

_____

To reach...

_____

GREAT POWER

To achieve greatness takes great power. As discussed in the previous chapter, it takes a great power to overcome, a great power to endure, a great power to change. It also takes a great power to stay with and trust one's own vision.

We all want positive changes in today's world, and we know those changes comes about through those who possess the power to make decisions. When we achieve greatness, we will find ourselves in the position where we are making decisions that create change. Those in positions of power become leaders who have special qualities that separate them from managers. A manager simply manipulates the means to an end. A leader is a guide toward progression who not only connects with and has a relationship with the group, but also models and inspires those who follow and who want to pick up the torch.

To lead is to have great power. In the context of seeking to reach impossible visions every day, one should strive to obtain the power it takes to bring about change. That power begins in the power of self: self-concept, self-determination, and self-discipline[3].

Self-Concept

Self-concept is defined as "a person's perception of his or her own strengths, weaknesses, abilities, attitudes, and values"[4]. Nathaniel Branden quotes, "The greatest barrier to achievement and success is not lack of talent or ability but rather the feeling that achievement and success, above a certain level, are outside our self-concept—our image of who we are and what is appropriate to us."

We all possess the power to do great things. What sets one person ahead of another is the level of drive that is fueled by the level of belief in self. Are you faster than a speeding bullet, more powerful than a locomotive, and able to leap buildings in a single bound? My guess is probably not, but you do have abilities that are unique to you that will move you toward reaching your goal.

Some people say that heroes are born. Others say that heroes are made. I tend to think that both hold true. Some people have natural abilities that they just excel at with seemingly little effort. Others have basic skills that they work on relentlessly until that basic skill turns into a professional ability. You have to figure out which one you are. Never take your natural ability for granted. You may not have to work as hard as the others, but eventually the others will catch up to you if you don't continue to cultivate your craft on a daily basis. It is your job to extend your ability to a level that you didn't think was possible. That is seeking to reach impossible visions every day. Your competition should be only to outdo your past self. Those who have to work at it must use their resources.

Of course I'm going to say that education is one of the greatest resources, but let me tell you why I believe that. I say that my superpower is being an educator. The reasoning follows the fact that I personally have acquired skills and abilities from school that has allowed me to arrive to the place that I stand today. My success in school gave me a choice in the career that I chose. Being that my education took me from poverty to success, I chose being an educator as a way to pay it forward. However, I have other extraordinary abilities. I like to talk, but I also like to do other things that I built through my language arts classes. I learned to speak well, which allowed me to become a motivational speaker. I also learned about literary devices that, put together, create these things called "spoken word" and "hip hop," which gave me the power to entertain. Not only do I use my verbal skills to be a motivational speaker and write and perform poetry and music, I also utilize the knowledge from history and social studies to make relevant references in my speeches and writings. Likewise, I like the mathematical skills that I acquired from my math class to be able count money and establish my own educational services business. I have new options of a future, careers, and ways to leave my memory behind; all stemming from the use of resources I gathered through the power of education.

What's your superpower? It can start as small as a hobby or something you like to do all the time. Everyone is capable of doing something, and capabilities become cape abilities. Cape abilities are born where your ordinary abilities become extraordinary abilities in the pursuit of greatness. However, you need to use your resources to expand these abilities; to make you extraordinary; to build your power. Remembering that power comes from within, we must reflect upon our actions to access the power.

 To guide the reflection process from the perspective of self-concept, ask yourself the following questions:

- What value do I have to others?

- What can I do today that would be of great value to someone else?

- What successful person stands as a concrete example of myself-concept? What qualities do we share? What qualities can I improve upon?

Self-Determination

Self-determination is defined as free choice of one's own acts or states without external compulsion[5]. Kilroy J. Oldster quotes, "Humankind's greatest gift is that we are indeterminate beings. Unlike the tough and leathery seed of an acorn, which will grow into a magnificent oak tree, none of us has a predetermined final configuration of our ultimate essence. Our mental temperament is pliable. We make conscious and subconscious choices that govern who we become."

To insert my interpretation of the previous quote, we can choose what we become, and we all possess the capacity to be what we want. However, we must be determined to reach the goals that we set. Our choices should not be a result of trying to fulfill someone else's vision of what we should be—they should be absent of outside influence. Our choices also must not be forced upon us due to our inability to act. We must prepare to take the initiative and take deliberate action in order live up to the definition of self-determination.

 To activate self-determination, reflect on the following questions:

- What is my goal for today? What is the first thing I will do to work on that goal?

- What is going to help me start my action steps? Are my actions from my own choice, or am I seeking permission or approval of others?

- Does the reaction of people to my choices or behaviors show a positive or negative value? If negative, what can I do differently to show positive value?

- Can I stick with my choice of action if it is different from others or if others express a different opinion?

Self-Discipline

Self-discipline is defined as the correction or regulation of oneself for the sake of improvement[6]. Sukant Ratnakar wrote, "Self-discipline is the only power which can keep you energized even in the toughest of the circumstances." Self-discipline is the greatest deterrent of distractions and procrastination. There is much good in having a positive self-concept (feeling good about who you are) and self-determination (relentless pursuit), but power and momentum can lead to great catastrophe when colliding with physical matter. In other words, one can have great drive to seek greatness through their self-concept and self-determination, but self-discipline is needed to avoid the obstacles.

Self-discipline keeps your eyes on the goal or on the path, despite the temptation to deviate, turn around, or stop. Self-discipline also sounds the alarm at the sign of choices that can be detrimental to your ultimate outcome. Self-discipline is the security and the fortitude to safeguard the journey. With the pressures of life from popular culture and peers, it is routinely a difficult process to stay on your own path without the urge to surrender to the influence. The greater the discipline one has, the easier it is to resist.

To build and maintain the power of self-discipline, reflect on the following questions:

- Can I analyze my behavior and make corrections without being prompted or influenced?

- Do I know what checks and balances I require to assess and regulate my behavior?

- What is my first response to keep me going when I recognize a challenge?

- Do my choices lead to positive outcomes?

S.T.R.I.V.E FOR GREATNESS

After reading this chapter, I will seek to...

_____
_____
_____
_____
_____
_____
_____
_____
_____
_____
_____
_____
_____
_____
_____

To reach...

_____
_____
_____
_____
_____
_____
_____
_____

GREAT RESPONSIBILITY

A famous line from one of the Spider-Man movies says, "With great power lies great responsibility." We have a responsibility as citizens of humanity to be a shining light in the world and not shading the world to darkness. Winston Churchill once said, "The price of greatness is responsibility." A great responsibility associated with humanity is to maintain one's power and use it for good. When you don't use your power for good, it just becomes a privilege. Privilege leads to prejudice, and prejudice, to racism. I'm not just talking about a certain race. I'm talking about people in general.

How do you ensure you're maintaining your power and using it for good? The three intrinsic factors of self-concept, self-determination, and self-discipline will begin to exude in outwardly traits of character, motivation, and perseverance. The handling of the previously stated traits will attest to the positive use of your power.

Character

Character is defined by the age-old adage, "what you do when no one is looking." It can further be viewed as the manifestation of your self-concept, meaning that it is the collective of your strengths, weaknesses, abilities, attitudes, and values at play. In a greater sense, it is the extent of consistency or inconsistency of your self-concept. The vision you have for yourself affects the decisions you make in the world.

As mentioned in the introduction, as you pursue the knowledge of what you want to do or who you want to be, you do so in the presence of others. What decisions you make informs others of your strengths, weaknesses, abilities, attitudes, and values; therefore, your decisions play a role in the formulation of what others perceive as your character. Also stated previously, the others are the ones who will build your statue. So it is important to build not only good character, but great character if you wish to witness the construction of your marker of greatness.

Motivation

Motivation is the force or eagerness to do or act[7]. Motivation is the fuel that feeds self-determination. As previously defined, self-determination is the choice of action without influence. The choice of action is the spark to begin the journey toward greatness. Once the choice is made, motivation keeps the flame burning. It takes a fire of desire to motivate us to seek the impossible. The term "impossible" may lead us to consider the action to unworthy of our effort. However, the light of self-determination fed with motivation will steer the engine straight into the unknown and on to the destination of greatness.

Perseverance

Perseverance is the continued effort to do or achieve something despite difficulties, failure, or opposition[8]. Perseverance can only be maintained through the continued use of regulation and correction that address difficulties, failures, or opposition. Regulation and correction are qualities of the self-discipline it takes to have unyielding effort.

If self-determination is the spark and motivation is the fuel, then self-discipline is the engine and perseverance is the engineer. The spark and the fuel work inside the engine to make it go. The engine is the vessel that contains the necessary processes to navigate the world. The engineer steers the engine about the terrain, adjusting to hills, valleys, obstructions, and cautions.

The definition of S.T.R.I.V.E. (seek to reach impossible visions every day) reflects the notion that the journey chosen is that which many would not think is worth the effort, or one they feel they have insufficient power to achieve. We can reach beyond those boundaries, using all of the components—character, perseverance, motivation—because they are important and should be in each of us in abundant amounts. Character can be seen as the parts to the engine, motivation is the fuel, and perseverance is the engineer. Together, each part completes the elements necessary to strive for greatness!

S.T.R.I.V.E FOR GREATNESS

After reading this chapter, I will seek to...

To reach...

GREAT EXPECTATIONS

With great power lies great responsibility. An understanding of power and responsibility reveals the necessity of expectations to guide the journey of *seeking to reach impossible visions every day*. There is a set of principles we must follow in order to maintain our focus on the vision. When we strive for greatness, we will effectively communicate the following five principles[9]:

1 **I must show empathy/compassion**

2 **Empathy/compassion is a part of belonging**

3 **We all should want success/happiness**

4 **Challenges show distinction, not defect**

5 **The future is now**

I Must Show Empathy/Compassion

As part of a commencement speech, renowned photographer Bill Bullard said, "The highest form of knowledge is empathy." Empathy is defined as the action of understanding, being aware of, being sensitive to, and vicariously experiencing the feelings, thoughts, and experience of another of either the past or present without having the feelings, thoughts, and experience fully communicated in an objectively explicit manner[10]. To reach an equal view of humanity and education, we must be sensitive to others' experiences.

Psychologist Carl Rogers wrote, "Each person is an island unto himself, in a very real sense; and he can only build bridges to other islands if he is first of all willing to be himself and permitted to be himself." The compassion and understanding created through empathy can bridge people together, establishing an equality of humanity and thus reaching the impossible vision—the vision that reveals greatness.

Empathy is achieved through understanding the context of others' thinking and actions. As I presented the context of my "why" in the Great Minds chapter, I aimed at helping readers begin to understand a larger context of African American people. I will also share other contexts in the final chapter, A Tribute to Greatness, to provide a greater understanding of my "why" beyond just my ethnicity. In doing so, I hope to set the example of not only communicating our own context so that others understand, but also seeking to learn about the context of others so that our own understanding increases. The result is the building of an essential component of greatness: empathy.

Empathy/Compassion Is a Part of Belonging

Not only is it important that we show empathy and compassion, but we also should surround ourselves with those who are capable of showing empathy and compassion. The human race has an innate desire to belong, and the acceptance of an individual into a particular circle is dependent upon what the individual adds to the group. Compassion and empathy should be abundant in any circle where we expect to receive support to help us strive for greatness.

The only way the bridge (referenced in the Carl Rogers quote) connects us is if we are connecting with like-minded individuals. Lack of empathy will burn a bridge and lead to isolation and marginalization—both qualities we find in the unfortunate "isms" that divide our society today. The measuring stick to determine the level of empathy in individuals with whom you surround yourself is their ability to say "I understand" and nothing else. If there are ifs, ands, or buts, their capacity for empathy and compassion is diminished. One should seek to belong to circles where empathy and compassion for others is a given.

We All (Should) Want Success/Happiness

The inward power to be great should also radiate an external responsibility to seek success and happiness. The desire fuels the drive, and we should assume that everyone wants both happiness and success. Our assumption works to decrease moments of contentment or idleness as well as allows management of the circle. The concept follows like-mindedness, in that those who do not wish to be successful should not dwell within the circle.

Such a mindset also creates the constructive competition that drives one to strive for greatness. Self-help writer Edmond Mbiaka said, "If you consistently surround yourself with winners, winning would become the only option in all your endeavors."

Challenges Show Distinction, Not Defect

Experiencing a difficult situation does not make one inadequate. Oftentimes, a challenge becomes the crossroads for the future. There are two choices: face the challenge or surrender to the challenge.

It has become a cliché to say that to be great, one must face challenges, but clichés are meant to be shared in exhaustion. However, I will add to the repetition that challenges are also important. When we look at history and how people react to fear, we see that the source of fear reflects a superiority and the relinquishing of power over a situation. When we relinquish power, we also lose knowledge of the outcome. In order to take back the power, we must conquer the fear and face the challenge.

It is important to also distinguish between true courage and false courage, or excuses. Excuses provide a false sense of accomplishment because we have successfully excused ourselves from the challenge, feeling as if it is an honorable dismissal. However, false courage is a form of fear and defeat, and we are relinquishing power when making excuses.

When faced with a challenge, we should only ask, "What strategies will it take to move forward?" The result shows the distinction between the mighty and the minute. To never make the decision to face a challenge is to surrender the journey to strive for greatness.

The Future Is Now

Now is the time to turn on the power and take the responsibility. Now is the time to take up the challenge to face difficulties. As the saying goes, "If you are early, you are on time; if you are on time, you are late; and if you are late, you should not have shown up." The future is now, so to get started is to be on time.

As you read these words, begin to make an action plan that initiates your journey to seek to reach impossible visions every day. After reading this chapter today, what will you do tomorrow that reflects the attitude of striving for greatness?

S.T.R.I.V.E FOR GREATNESS

After reading this chapter, I will seek to...

_____
_____
_____
_____
_____
_____
_____
_____
_____
_____
_____
_____
_____
_____

To reach...

_____
_____
_____
_____
_____
_____
_____

STRIVING FOR GREATNESS

Consistent communication of the great expectations explained in the previous section is evidence of the journey toward greatness. The process is a great challenge, but it leads to great accomplishments. Reaching the impossible visions gives new meaning to success and shows a renewed focus on possible outcomes.

The person who matters the most when determining if you have reached greatness is yourself. Trying to keep up with others is a moving target. Face it, we would hope that every single individual on earth is on a journey to greatness. In actuality, it may not be every single person, but I can also predict that the number will be significant. So, it is important to set the standard of greatness in our own definition of self-actualization, contentment, and happiness.

I would also measure greatness in the value we add to our community or society as a whole, as it been stated that greatness is a by-product of the efforts to achieve equality of humanity. To further explore measures of greatness, I have compiled what I term "Markers of Greatness." They act as benchmarks or summative assessments of goal setting in the journey to reach the impossible visions.

Looking back at the Strive Chain chapter, here is where the determination of where the ceremony or the rite of passage starts—where we know we are at the figurative presentation of our token of achievement. To know that we are achieving on extraordinary measures, we can use the following Markers of Greatness:

Aspiration v. Attainment

Closing the gap between aspiration and attainment is a marker that shows when we approaching greatness. Many of us aspire to carry out some goal in life; however, the lengths we go to attain the goal, and the extent to which we attain or exceed the goal, is a measure of greatness. Aspire not simply to set goals, but also to dream big. Then, wake up and seek the impossible visions so that you reach the pinnacle of greatness!

Falsify Negative Generalizations

A huge measure of greatness is the ability to falsify negative generalizations. This marker is a persistent motivator in my personal journey toward greatness. The world is full of those who make rash judgments, inaccurately place a set of stigmas on social groups, or simply lack faith in the potential of individuals to excel. Many lack the knowledge to make educated deductions, and some lack the desire to acquire the knowledge. The lack of desire leads to an instant output of negative generalizations. However, striving for greatness means one is seeking the vision that can counteract the generalizations. It also means having the self-determination and self-discipline to create and maintain your path to success, unyielding to the influences of others—

motivation in your own image. A measure of greatness is to stand on your own individual accomplishments or characteristics and stand out from common generalizations, especially the negative.

Create Your Own Image

This marker of greatness also can be seen as an extension of falsifying negative generalizations. After we counteract the negative generalizations that have been associated with a particular group or idea, we create our own unique images that separate from the pack. Be an innovator! Creating your own image means to seek to reach impossible visions on your own terms. True power lies in the ability to control situations by personal actions and decisions, not succumbing to the opinions of others. When you create your own image, you do not waste precious time and energy walking in the shadows of others or trying to reach unrealizable expectations. In both cases, you're at a disadvantage, being positioned behind others instead of leading the pack. Greatness is the ability to be a great leader.

Engage in the Unknown

This marker of greatness is dependent upon the confidence and courage gained through great power and responsibility. To reiterate a powerful notion, if your dreams do not scare you, they are not big enough. We previously discussed the idea that many fall to the power of the unknown and even replace their thinking with a false confidence that giving up was the best decision, rather than confronting the fear. The measure of greatness is determined by your ability to face those fears and address them with confidence, determination, and discipline. Engaging in the unknown is the essence of seeking to reach impossible visions. Change does not come in comfort. Engaging in the unknown is definitely not comfortable, so we will certainly come out a changed individual. We seek to have the change documented as a marker of greatness!

After reading this chapter, I will seek to...

To reach...

GREAT WISDOM - THE SUMMARY

A lot of information has been presented in a diverse fashion, and the question on your mind might be, "What is he trying to communicate in simple fashion?" Here are a few common wisdoms I would like to leave with you:

❶ Great Minds remind us to seek education to achieve equal humanity

❷ Great Power
- Seek self-worth
- Seek the drive to excel
- Seek will power and restraint

❸ Great Responsibility
- Seek credibility
- Seek impetus
- Seek endurance

❹ Great Expectations
- Reach empathy
- Reach community
- Reach initiative
- Reach impossible visions

❺ Striving for Greatness
- Reach a foundation of hope
- Reach the other side of challenges

A TRIBUTE TO GREATNESS

My "Why"

I was born in a small town in Alabama and raised in public housing projects by a single mom with eight children. I saw struggles at an early age. Meals were at a minimum; we would accept any handouts we could get. We lived by convenience, having to walk most places, including stores and doctors. I'm sure you can imagine all the things that go along with being poor.

In my youth, I would have been categorized as "at-risk" for not being successful. I found myself conflicted in my motivation. On one hand, I listened to those who said that my education was most important, and I excelled in school. On the other hand, I was motivated by my surroundings and lived almost a double life between school and home, as I chose to participate in things my mother probably would not be too proud of to this day.

I graduated from high school with honors and tens of thousands if not more in scholarships (including full ride scholarships from institutions and the military). However, the conflict between my education and personal choices led me to becoming a college dropout and a participant in multiple temp service jobs, including scooping sawdust and working in a graveyard. However, as fortune would be granted, I sat at a college waiting for someone else to go on a campus tour (in which

I had no personal interest) and would leave with my own scholarship offer on site. Thus I began a pivotal turn in my life.

It was the moment I stepped onto the campus that my vision began to clear. I began to seek more and go beyond my past experiences. I can truly say that I began my journey to seek to reach impossible visions on a daily basis. Perhaps you can also see why I can stand behind the belief of seeking education. It was from this particular moment in my life where I began to write, perform, speak, and advocate for others who are viewed as "at risk." I began to strive for greatness.

When it comes to striving for greatness, I have always been motivated to do so based on my image and profession. Think about this: I am an African American male from a single-parent family of eight children living in public housing. I have dreads and for a while drove around in an all-black car with tint and black rims. I write, record, and perform spoken word and hip hop. Additionally, I am an assistant principal at a high school with a doctorate in education. I am also a proud and active member of Phi Beta Sigma Fraternity, Inc, a historically black Greek letter organization.

There is much to say about the image related to the attributes of which I previously stated. Being an African American male from the projects, who has dreads and drives an all-black car with rims probably would stir negative stereotypical images of a "thug." The fact that I rap would seemingly insinuate that I wish to be a "gangster rapper." It is a stark difference from one who has a doctorate degree. Even more, the image of being a member of a fraternity can have its own pre-conceived notions. However, part of my striving for greatness was a process of ensuring I was accepted for all that I am.

I did not ask to be born in poverty, but it taught me survival and it allowed me to relate to those of which I come into contact that have similar stories. I embraced the culture of hip hop and spoken word as an expression to channel my feelings in a positive way. I leaned on my education to enhance those interests so that others would be interested in my talents. I am a big proponent of historically black Greek letter organizations because they can often be misrepresented, but their purpose is rich and contributed in my journey towards greatness. These institutions and organizations are open to all races and ethnicities. They build on telling stories that establish attitudes that become culture. They stand as evidence of why education should matter to African Americans. They were established as academic and social institutions to fight for equal access to education and equality in humanity.

Reflecting on where I began and the knowledge that I gained has always sparked my motivation to seek impossible visions every day and to create them in my own vision. After navigating through what I call *"My Why,"* one would see the reflection of Great Minds, Great Power, Great Responsibility, and Great Expectations that I established for myself so that I could S.T.R.I.V.E. for Greatness. What follows is the product of what I explained as a major turning point in my life. As those elements of seeking to reach impossible visions every day began to come together, my interests in spoken word, hip hop, and even performing and speaking began to flourish. As I conclude the book, I present my *My Works*, a compilation of poetry and lyrics inspired by my life and enriched by my journey to S.T.R.I.V.E for Greatness.

My Works

A Tribute to Greatness

I watched a show recently on BET that cut me deeply,

Causing me to bleed emotions and bereave

To know that we as a people die more today

Than the martyrs raised in the fruit trees

Or the birds caged according to Dr. Angelou.

And with the report of a songbird that has been separated body from soul,

She quotes how we compete with hate in a footrace by crossing lines of self-degradation

That we claim as a language, filled with slang and slur.

It has not occurred to our youth that the fear of knowledge mastered in the slave days

Has been transformed to peer expectations that portray the definition of cool.

And as the songbird sang, the children are our future, give them a sense of pride,

We must guide them back through the past to revive the vision our ancestors provide,

Bowed down, eyes watching God, their backs building the stepping stones,

S.T.R.I.V.E FOR GREATNESS

Their shoulders for generations to stand on so that we could touch the sky.
So why does one have to die to appreciate life when living is given at no price.

And even sacrifice has been made in time to create better days,
Just to be repaid with an illegal blow to the race
When our young men's pants hang below the waist.
You don't need your pants on the ground when people have lain down and gave their souls,
Committed their bodies to the ground to fertilize our future
We must take root and bear fruit in the image of a strong legacy;
Not reinstate the mentality of being a lesser being through perceived ignorance,
But achieving what the songbird sings as the greatest love of all—learning to love yourself
Because the power of prosperity and greatness lies within.

The Statutes of Liberty

As I watched the Inauguration of President Barack Obama mixed in with the air of history and remembrance of Dr. Martin Luther King, Jr., I was moved to pose a charge to the generation that I currently teach, placing my personal story as the centerpiece of building a dream, believing in it, and relentlessly persevering until the dream is a reality. After being inspired by the resounding words of President Obama, "With passion and dedication, let us answer the call of history and carry into an uncertain future that precious light of freedom," I give you an original poem titled "The Statutes of Liberty."

If I can't make you believe, then I'll just let you see
The blessings resting in the hands of the least of these;
Open palms like karate; no commodities;
Just empty hope held close with embraces, bracing through poverty;
Looking like that one man they can't stand
So they lock doors, hide keys
While he gazes back between locks and brown skin, with three degrees.
If I can't make you believe, then I'll just let you see
How he navigated through the streets of the Chattahoochee
Also known as the bricks, public housing, or the projects
With prospects of being just a statistic, until he went pro.

S.T.R.I.V.E FOR GREATNESS

Don't get it flipped, though, because it's no game;
It is success, gift-wrapped with a bow.

You wouldn't believe how you can go eight deep in sibling
rivalry,
With one apparent referee,
A single-parent left to be the figure both motherly and fatherly;
Now he's scholarly, called on to be the voice of reason;
Rising above and going beyond myth to man,
To stand at podiums, with all witnessing with their own eyes
the beliefs that speaks reality,
To bring you these, the Statutes of Liberty.

I.

Be young at heart, but wise in mind,
Compassionate in deed and speech,
Careful in wishful thinking,
Intentional in whom you groom to be.

II.

Be calculated in your time of action,
Take initiative, not invitation
Be daring in your destination,
Going beyond the beaten path;
Cut through the mountainous experience,
That the rocky terrain causes the mold to be shattered
thereafter.

III.

Build your dreams on faith, hope and love;

Leaving materials to their sole purpose;

Brick and mortar—the start of foundation, not for idolization

Because even buildings get dilapidated;

The man of steel still has his kryptonite;

But the will to drive with perseverance is the strength that lasts

beyond the ages.

Sticks and stones can spark fire to ignite a passion and desire,

And the prize shall come in the end,

Knowing that the bruises only scratch the surface,

Revealing the real you deep within.

Now take these statutes and you too will believe that you can be

of humble beginnings,

And see your dreams materialize before your eyes.

Then I won't have to make you believe,

You will see that what stands before you is the reality;

That one man,

From poverty and project streets,

To degrees, success and liberty,

Who believes…?

And I believe in each of you.

Succeed so that you may live free.

Do I Look Suspicious?

Do I look suspicious?
Is it because my pigment's tinted darker than the legal limit
Or my swagger is a natural cadence
Much less calculated than the footsteps waiting to give chase
Is my face not welcomed in my hood, in my place of residence?
Is it relevant to say that I was wasted?
When, face it,
So were you
With deadly force and endorphins
Racing with the notion that I fit your profile
Then apparently
Your goggle vision gave you the appearance of an imminent
threat
But your brain didn't get the memo
So you go pursue a threat in retreat
And catch heat from the attempt to subdue
And with desperate regret cry aggressor
And what we're left with
Is no justice, no peace
Cause it was just us,
One piece,
A young man lying in the street with skittle and tea
And the other man lying in wait to take a life and fly free

With no remorse

The young man, no voice

But with petition demands to be justified

Why life can be placed in the hands of a man

That thinks I look suspicious.

Cinderblock memories

Cinderblock memories building animosity

But I rise like a rose out of concrete

Lord knows I don't wanna be trapped in these walls

So he blessed me with flows that have set me free

I see reflections of a young boy standing in the window

Staring at his peers;

Through fear he trembles with social anxiety

Knowing he could never be part of them;

Cast down in a lower bracket;

Looking up at heaven and asking why he feels so alone;

Even with a fruitful home of eight;

And his mother carried weight like the bag lady,

So sure she hurt her back;

With heavy loads on each shoulder and still more to drag;

Now I vow to pick up the slack;

Trying to tighten the grip with graced lyrics;

Transmitting my soul and spirit in words like space satellites;

But they could not contain my range;

You can't picture my pain unless you can paint murals;

My consumption by a hard life feeding the fuel;

I composed these jewels in free verses from the high pressure of
the dirt until I struck diamonds;

With enough shine to spark fires with the rhymes, but I'm still
undiscovered;

My purpose is to show the price of struggle;

When triumph over trials causes my cup to run over;

Whether its wealth or contentment, I know that it's heaven sent;

Twenty-four years carried through the storms;

I received less love from my father than from strangers' arms;

But I still remained strong from the power walks; because I
never had an easy ride

I fought my way through the poverty and am still battling;

Straddling the fence of excelling or conforming;

Beating the pavement every morning; for every destination;

With no patience to escape Trap City;

Then I entered higher learning, still dreaming but returning to
the slums every summer;

Watching the pain collect in my mama's eyes and putting a
strain on my heart;

Wanting to be free ever since I saw the Klan march;

But that was just the start of overcast days;

Even the administration stole my grades in an attempt to steal
my mind, but I wouldn't have it;

My determination would not be outlasted;

Savage authorities bit off more than they could chew,
conspiring as if I was a threat like Huey P.;

But there was not much that they could do to me;

S.T.R.I.V.E FOR GREATNESS

I'm still here with volatile syllables that fill ears every time I
share my thoughts;
And I won't stop until substance in your cup spills and my
story is world renowned.

Corners (Remix)

Our corner mentality has shattered dreams like broken bottles
in back alleys,
But being black barely means we have to hold the streets down;
Chris Columbus proved the world was round so we can
circumnavigate the stereotypes.
But no matter right from wrong, we still feel the repercussions;
Sending us to the edge much like the Reaper's customs;
But it goes deeper; dusting the dirt and ashes as we rise like the
phoenix above the surface of the earth.
And we take flight above the street lights of street life;
Trying to beat the strife in a discreet plight to prove ourselves;
That we can escape the cells of our blocks
To no longer be locked down, or pinned by the state; or coined
by fate to have a 25 percent survival rate
We must raise the stakes like vampire slayers, or shine like the
sun to evaporate the blood thirsty;
And not will the spill of BP disasters;
But show that black people can master the universe, the world,
our cities, and our blocks.
That we leave fables for our future generations like Aesop;
Tales as noble as the knights at the round table of Camelot;
Not cornered, but holding weapons of Excalibur.
Weapons of knowledge that our ancestors, our brothers and

S.T.R.I.V.E FOR GREATNESS

sisters

Come from a long line of honored names on street signs

That landmark the maps each time they're spoken; showing that

we are not bound by

But identify that we own these streets.

Mysteries of Life Installment 1: Start with a goal

You hear the grown folks saying it; they keep on relaying the message and you take it and relay it; pass it on like a baton to the next one and give up the stride; because your pride and pop culture blocks you from the finish line.

Too bad, because you had the competition by a nose; but the notion is seemingly more abundant as if we frequent Neverland; where Lyfe quotes that nobody wants to grow old.

So many people think they got it but can't begin to visualize the size and magnitude to stake the claim; with hare-brained schemes of reality; trying to be the biggest fool on TV; Or the unrealistic villain of the community; Or revealing fruit that only a select few should have access to; Or being dangerous liaisons to weapons of man's destruction; causing bodily harm or brain damage. You probably couldn't handle it; though it seems reserved for the young.

You see, it starts with a goal; a target to mark the finish line or the rainbow to find that pot of gold; that elusive concept that grips the minds and desires as it proves status in the eyes of the mainstream. It is a stand that is rock solid or a walk that turns relativity on its ear; creating ripples in space, time and conformity to common law and mimicry.

It starts with a goal.

S.T.R.I.V.E FOR GREATNESS

So take hold of your ambitions and use persistence and discipline at full steam; clinging to your values and self-made path; not trampling on debris of those trying to lead you to obscurity; it's a command of style and grace where being notorious is no biggie.

It starts with a goal.

So take those four words in sequence as the acrostic to understand what you get is not handed; it's earned; once you've learned it, you've broken the barrier to acquisition of what all say they have but are truly missing; they say the lead but they lag with the absence of it…what do you have?

Strange Wisdoms

We find knowledge as a lesson,
Taught that it's a blessing,
Confessing our transgressions,
Consequences stating messages
Setting truth as our liberty
Mutual to the tears of reality
Indeed it may be actual
But far removed from tactful
We're brutal in our honesty
Barbaric in value
Literal interpretations,
And final in first impressions
Self-centered in our intentions
Too much to mask our prejudice
Our pride is superficial
And bordering detrimental
We know it, but yet ignore it
Strange wisdoms of our condition
Self-inflicted and cataclysmic
The catalyst to our destruction

The Seed

I want to live through my poetry
so will me into existence
because I thrive in metacognitions
through the transmission of my words
through your soul and spirit
just for you to see it, hear it, and feel it
gives nourishment to the seed of my imagination
fostering the germination of creativity
as you take part in the creation of my gift
and stand as gods among men and women

Diamond in the Rough

I started out thinking I was digging in a gold mine.

And found out that I was working in a coal mine.

I couldn't hold my mind's peace until I'm released from this graveyard shift.

My pastor told me to pray for my gift;

And no longer be a cave man;

It's my soul that needs saving;

And so I gave in;

All in as to call the devil's bluff;

Never thought I'd be that diamond in the rough;

A rich treasure lost among the perils of life;

Snatched back and then put on a pedestal;

And looking past the petty bull

And hearsay of what I used to be; never respecting who I am;

Who I'll remain is to claim the reign of terror is over;

I'm forever; a national treasure;

With enough strength to cut glass; and still be a girl's best friend.

Visions of Rapture

We all have our take on life and most agree that it doesn't treat
us right;
Wondering if there is a need to fight it;
Pledging allegiance to hold the strife close to my heart;
And made to believe that it's a right;
But when it bleeds, who makes it all right and who holds the
knife?
Or are they just one and the same? Or do we all share in the
blame?
Because we claim that we share in pain even though we travel
different planes;
Some soaring and some getting caught up in the world trade;
Like it's been gotten from the mind of bin Laden; but we've
been plotting our own downfall.
It's like we hate ourselves and it's no better when we get older;
That's why you can never find me sober;
Trying to distort reality to transform it around my goggle
vision.

I knew a girl who let the pressures around her close in;
Until she had no room for friends;
So packed tightly that she couldn't see over; didn't know love
rested on her shoulders

With wide open arms to hold her to keep her warm so her heart
grew colder;
And I told her that I was everything that she needs,
But I don't know why the pain still collects in her eyes;
You can't disguise strength with foolish pride;
I didn't want to be a ruler or guide; just a confidant to help ease
the ride
While rolling shotgun beside her;
You only got one life to live; one love to give
That is made of pure emotion; the rest is hoping for fulfillment
to voids;
Which can only be filled by God;
But we still rely on ourselves, making our lives a living hell,
And the price of bail is our soul;
One precious piece that I hope to hold until my days of old.
So that I reach the rays of gold that reach from the sky.
No more signing a lease but inheriting my place in heaven.
And cop a plea that my past be irrelevant; when I indulged in
all three of the seven deadly sins;
I would have severed heads for friends or broken
commandments,
But in the end I'm the one condemned; I can't be saved by them;
So what's the worth of the risk?
Not enough to continue so I stick to my own venues,
Looking for visions of rapture to take my soul to the life after.

S.T.R.I.V.E FOR GREATNESS

Dear God,

Make me a bird

So I can fly high and maybe even touch the sky

Because the devil can't catch me when I'm rising

But the ghosts can't catch me when I fall

So I'm waiting on you to come take me away.

I've Realized...

I've realized that there's no compromise in life
Compiling the awards won't stack up to the strife;
With your back to the knife, you can't combat the plight of a
backstabber's strike
Unless you take your sword and slice your own piece of the pie.
No one can see through my eyes because my point of view is
egocentric.
We may be co-written with the will of God, but we still set the
sparks to his light.

To ignite a notion to strike with a harmonious blow we must
wise up and realize that
We are living vicariously but we don't need them to carry us.
Lead your own life and don't let anyone try to stop you.
And if they do, you must be prepared to fight.
We have the right to remain violent; we don't move in silence,
we incite riots;
Liable to invoke the biased and the prejudiced by demanding
justice;
Holding blunt objects to heart of the cowards who try to devour
our will to live.

Home Coming...

(Dedicated to my grandmother, Susie Anna; R.I.P.)

Have no sorrows because the sun sets
And this side of the world settles to a silent rest
Because the dawn of a new day brings fresh light
Unseen to us, but still it's all right
Through the trust in God's promises
On the other side, the sun will give rise to new life.
In a place that's a world away but near in our hearts
One journey's done, but a new one starts;
Don't be torn apart,
But be sworn to pardon the harsh hand life deals;
Feel blessed to know that love heals;
Above hills of green pastures faint laughter resounds;
Even though down here we mourn.
Just know they're home and the struggle is over;
Reach out and grab a shoulder
Don't be afraid to let loved ones hold you
They're the glue to mend and mold you.
And only God has control of what goes on;
All we can do is hold on and stay strong;
And know that we'll be together one day
Just where we belong.

Untitled

(Dedicated to Camp Promise)

I'm trying to find my way back…way back;

Like the echoes delayed in the sound wave track;

Because I found that yesterday makes the history that entertains our tomorrow

Whenever we push the playback.

It's the days that were most unbearable that contain the parable to construct our knowledge.

Though abrupt, it's a solid foundation to the nature of memorable moments.

So I hold on to the past and try to find my way back…way back,

When it wasn't wrong to say that today was a good day.

The children play outside while I sit and collect the rhyme from inside my spirit;

And compose a piece of work to move people to tears;

It's been years ago up to the present that this essence has elevated my style;

Up to the moment I received a smile back from the kids as I kept a watchful eye.

It's such inspiration that my pen generates the feeling of joy as I reach back…

Way back in the past to make the times last forever; getting past

S.T.R.I.V.E FOR GREATNESS

the weather;

We may have had stormy nights, but the sun still rose in the morning;

A fresh new day dawned, portrait drawn, and chapter written in ways we will never forget;

Even though in a split second it's all over.

But we grab on to the past and get back to the good old days, after we have parted ways,

By reaching way back to the place inside our hearts that safeguards those precious pieces of life.

So let's get back…way back…and take advantage of the events that have made this poem a collected memory.

Better Days

Better days come as often as a tsunami;
This is an incredible wave of true honesty;
You humbly bow down to what is predestined;
Investing in the positives of what is expected;
Neglecting the signs in your line of sight
To face the brutality when it stabs like a steel knife
Because it's still night and we can never still life
Like the masterpieces that exaggerate what is real life.

But we take the pain and move on
Reconstruct the strand of DNA that makes us strong
It takes a long time and the price is hard to be appraised
But it's worth it when we find the better days
As mellow waves flow through our minds
When the rays from the sun reach down and lift us up to
heaven
Like the seventh sign completing the cycle
We can all be street disciples; it only takes a moment
To spread the word of how surviving the hard life leads to
paradise
A different world and we all can own it.

P.O.W.E.R.
(Prove Our Worth, Earn Respect)

They telling me that I'm free
I'm trying to live but I can't breathe
My hands up, they shoot me
I can't kneel but they take a knee
On my neck

Getting respect by any means
And that's on X
Cause it marks where they chained me
400 years and I ain't free
Just changed the language like text to speech
From three-fifths compromise to black Wall Street

Our black lives don't matter
Till window panes are shattered
But they rather mend windows than the pain that they rendered
upon me
How about that humanity
Flags over mortality...don't value me
But I'll make you value me
By any means

The state labeling me like I'm the enemy
Supremacy feed legislation to the chief

The system wasn't made for me

I was born black didn't make it up like Maybelline

I'ma prove our worth and earn respect and that's on me

Power over tyranny

They feel me or fear me

Either way it's victory over enemies

Systemic inequities and police brutality

But we gone get this power.

A Resurrected King

I march to the rhythm of the Negro spirituals;
Singing ancestral songs of sorrow, detailing our rituals;
Lifting our heads to the almighty while bending down in the
fields of hard labor and harsh conditions.
Not to extract cotton and crops of ancient masters,
But to uproot the present seeds of hatred that have sprouted in
the hearts of our fellow human beings.
Like Martin Luther King I want to cultivate the nightmare of
reality into a new dream;
A dream that can be instilled in the minds of all; without one
plotting the others' fall.

We are all guilty of allowing the redness of anger and violence
to filter through our minds through the demand and desire for
equal rights,
While our better half fluctuates between dim yellow hues of fear
and green and envious eyes, mad to see that we can overcome.
This makes us to be a naïve world.
Because so many pigments filter through the whole screen of
the black and white scene,
Yet we cannot see our future to be multicultural.
However the mixture is there.
We must allow the colors to transform to more constructive fill-

ins to our hearts

And not sketch destructive thoughts in our minds.

The Hip Hop of my Soul

I know that it's a part of me;

Breaking shackles with my bare hands until I free verses of expressions

With the progression of a rhythm

For you to absorb through your pores

Because it's more to it than for you to just hear them

I start with sixteen bars to swing on with irregular melody,

Mixed in end rhyme in couplets;

Free verses and even a few curse words;

Stream of conscience to a meter from the baseline;

Metaphorical insinuations and innuendos;

Lyrical literal prose;

Composed through meditation or free-styled;

Printed or performed;

A fusion and metamorphosis;

Consistent in its incineration of the spirit, the mind…

Soul.

My People

My people we need to start dreaming. Let's start dreaming.
Because we're waking up and realizing our demise with them
eyes that watch us every time we go to the corner store to get
our favorite kind of Cheetos.
There goes another one chasing after my son, trying to make it
so he can't shine.
And the ghost-face dropping the dime 'til he winds up further
in poverty, other people's property; no it's not mine.
Tell me is this freedom.
Or is it just an illusion of the fusion of mankind starting in Eden
to Babylon to Amistad to Montgomery all the way to Callaway.
How much the world has changed today! But the chains still
remain and the stain of melanin in the skin seems to add
shadow to the soul but not in mine.
I don't walk that line, but I'm not blind.
My pride is not a handicap or a lack of will.
It is the strength of steel that runs through my veins.
I don't walk that line, but I'm not blind.
Yet I fail the criteria and mass hysteria intoxicates my limbs till I
am bound, face down in chains because my name can't light the
brain.
I'm still searching for my fame.
But in the next five minutes I'm printed and booked and from

the looks of it I'm about to become known.

My people, that's how we've grown today but there has to be a better way to leave our mark.

Because the world don't decipher in the dark. Its sends out blind shots till silhouettes stand still

And then peel away the rubble in the early dawn. Now my whole family is gone, taken away by the world trying to do us in.

Looked upon us as if we are sin.

We can't win to begin so we end speculation with expectations of stereotypical trends and then, do ourselves in.

Oh Lord just stop the spins; the cycle turning our lives upside-down, side-out, defensive and aggressive, ghetto and proud.

Living in the word "derogatory" and wondering why we can't rise.

Because the load multiplies with the eyes of your third-born child.

The ratio 1 to 4, smiles to frowns, because you're still down and you can't rise. Because the load multiplies with the eyes of a violent child.

Living a prescribed lifestyle but it's not mine.

My people we need to start dreaming.

Even though we may toss and turn it shows us to be alive.

And as we strive to be seen in a new light, we often paint our own predicaments and pre-conceived indictments lie awaiting to eclipse our glow.

Oh no, the night is nigh. We become the pupil of the world's eye; the pigment that identities.

And who am I? I am the next King to bring to us a dream to illuminate.

Twilight doesn't mean too late. It means through our darkness lets radiate.

That all the world looks up to the night and wish upon our celestial light to also be nocturnal.

Not to be like us, but one with us and in the morning we wake up to the reality that we are all God's children.

ABOUT THE AUTHOR

Dr. Nigel L. Walker was born February 13, 1980, to David and Jacqueline T. Walker. He was born and raised in Eufaula, AL, along with seven brothers and sisters. Jacqueline raised all eight children as a single mother in the public housing projects throughout his childhood. He began writing at an early age, and published his first poetry book, The Secret Diaries of Jean Batiste in 2004. His follow-up, Rose Petals for Josephine: The Secret Diaries Volume II was released in 2007. He also published a narrative nonfiction work entitled The Underground Philosophy of Education: Teaching is Not for Dummies in 2011.

Dr. Nigel L. Walker earned his Bachelors, Masters, and Specialist degrees in Education all at LaGrange College in LaGrange, GA. He earned his Doctorate at Columbus State University in Columbus, GA. Dr. Walker currently serves as a high school assistant principal. He is also member of the alternative hip hop recording group, *Hypoetically Speaking*, and a motivational speaker. He resides in LaGrange, GA with his wife and four daughters.

SPECIALTY/SERVICES

Professional Development / Training

- Teacher Leadership Training
- Curriculum and Instruction
- Collaborative Leadership
- Family Advocate
- Growth Mindset
- School Culture and Diversity
- Positive Behavior Interventions and Support
- School Climate
- Consulting Services
- Restorative Discipline

Mentoring

- Teacher Advisory/Mentoring
- Academic Identities
- Service Learning
- STRIVE Mentoring Program
- Character Education

Motivational Speaking

- STRIVE for Greatness
- Personal Identity
- Poetry/Hip Hop Performance/Presentations
- Power of Education
- Community Activism

S.T.R.I.V.E FOR GREATNESS

For more information or to contact Dr. Nigel L. Walker

🌐   www.willedservices.com

ⓕ   @nlwalker

🐦   @jbatiste3d

📷   @willedservices, @j_doc_batiste, @hypoeticallyspeaking

Merchandise available in S.T.R.I.V.E. Store of Classic Culture
Brand: linktr.ee/classicculturebrand

ACKNOWLEDGMENTS

1. Dweck CS. *Mindset: The New Psychology of Success.* Ballantine Books; 2006.

2. Greenberg J. Six reasons I want my white child to take ethnic studies. In: *Rethinking Ethnic Studies.* Rethinking Schools; 2019:293-299.

3. Whiting G. The Scholar Identity Institute: Guiding Darnel and other Black Males. *Gift Child Today.* 2009;32(4):53-63. doi:10.1177/107621750903200413

4. Slavin RE. *Educational Psychology: Theory and Practice.* 3rd ed. Pearson; 2003.

5. Self-determination | Definition of Self-determination by Merriam-Webster. Accessed May 17, 2020. https://www.merriam-webster.com/dictionary/self-determination

6. Self-discipline | Definition of Self-discipline by Merriam-Webster. Accessed May 17, 2020. https://www.merriam-webster.com/dictionary/self-discipline

7. Motivation | Definition of Motivation by Merriam-Webster. Accessed May 17, 2020. https://www.merriam-webster.com/dictionary/motivation

8. Perseverance | Definition of Perseverance by Merriam-Webster. Accessed May 17, 2020. https://www.merriam-webster.com/dictionary/perseverance

9. Oyserman D. *Pathways to Success Through Identity-Based Motivation.* Oxford University Press; 2015.

10.   Empathy | Definition of Empathy by Merriam-Webster. Accessed May 17, 2020. https://www.merriam-webster.com/dictionary/empathy

CPSIA information can be obtained
at www.ICGtesting.com
Printed in the USA
LVHW081511260321
682585LV00029B/345